PAGES OF

Plenty

MASHAO JORDAN

PAGES OF PLENTY

For permissions, contact:
Mashao Jordan
pagesofplenty@gmail.com

Cover Design and Interior Formatting by Rein G.
Illustrations by Rein G.
@reindrawthings (www.fiverr.com)

ISBN: 979-8-9995688-0-9 (Paperback)
ISBN: 979-8-9995688-1-6 (Hardcover)
ISBN: 979-8-9995688-2-3 (Ebook)

First Edition

Printed in the United States of America

Printed by Amazon KDP
Published by Independently Published

This book is for
YOU.

TABLE OF CONTENTS

- CHAPTER I -

Love

With You Always

All inclusive

Infinite years

Of exclusive bliss

Despite what we have missed

I still can't picture

A lifetime without

You

Some old

And some new

But it all

Is everlasting

Is honored

Is valued

Is true

You have resurrected

My life

And I yours

We have opened doors

Toward each other

Forward

We have adored our past

And built new perspectives

On

At last

You asked

Me

What is the meaning

Of life

It's

I'm on my way

To you

It's

My first thought

And last longing

It's peeling back the layers

Growing and belonging

With you

It's ongoing
Odes to you
The meaning of life is
Finding where you are
And leaping into continuum
The meaning is optimum
When you're involved
The meaning of life is
Towards
Upward, onward, forward
With you

Travelers

We took long walks
Through future plans
We drove by fields
That could fertilize
Our seeds
We traveled through
Time
We took a train
Going fast toward
Forever
Biking endlessly down
Lovers lane
We turned right
On union circle
We strolled barefoot
In the rain
We whispered words
Of affirmation
We became
Wanderlust lovers
We wandered
We wondered
Where to next

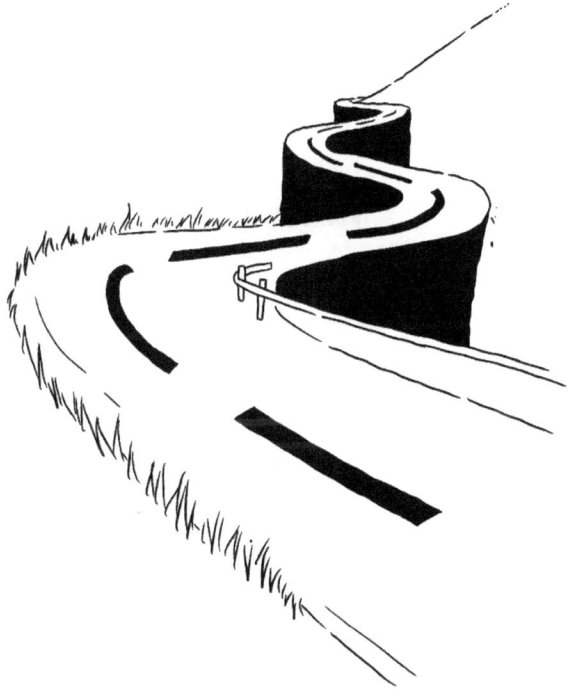

For You

I
Can't pretend anymore
There's only one way out in a dead end
And that's the way you came
And when I came, I had nothing
Leave my past to be the blame
When instead it's me
Making the same mistakes twice
While living in vain -- But still...
Praying I hope to one day see
The clouds open up and
The heavens rain down upon me
In you
I wanted to see the Heavens
In you
And that's where my actions
Became plain blasphemy of my conscience
What I thought to be love
My deepest breath, my last drink of life
The second beat of my heart
To this song we all search for
Vanished
I realized you were gone
And just as quickly as you came at that

As quickly as I came back
Time and time again, trying to understand
What even being in life's class early
Couldn't teach me
That even the deepest breath of fresh air
Can kill you just the same
That the moment your heart
Skips that beat
You yearn to make up for your shortcomings
To prove yourself
To understand
Why you equally can't stand
The feeling you long for
Deep down in your soul
LOVE

Soulmate

There's patience inside time
And riding on faith is life's true journey
Longing, just for you to learn me
I make mistakes
But allow my feelings to turn me
Down what is now
A no outlet
My heart concerns me
See I've breathed all the air I can
And I'm ready to hold my breath now
Stopping time, I'm holding tight
To this one journey
With two hands protecting it
I peek sometimes
Waiting to glimpse the surface of
What I hope to find
So, with truth in mind
I let you inside
And now "in" becomes inside out
And mostly doubt left
I'm out my right mind
Fighting my pride
Which exposes all open spaces
Meanwhile comfort changes overnight

Like bills with big faces

And what was mystery, I have given to you

Past spirit

And safe keeping becomes my worry

Because now

Truth, well I fear it

I fear that in fact

You may not stay

And such frustration coming endlessly

From being forced to walk away

Leaving my heart with you

See, even ordinary people

Can become strangers and some lovers become friends

But soulmates, well

They'll either be together or

To uncertainty give in

I think of you, often

Hoping that all the small things

Are counting for you

Meanwhile, I'm praying to God

To keep you from meeting my past

And hoping that if this is

Just a learning experience

Well hoping that the learning,

Is what lasts
See, my reality clouds
Create shadows that forecast the future
Presenting the presence of being left alone
In mind, spirit and in soul
And what I disregarded so easily before
Has come back to haunt me
And I'm not in control anymore
I realize I've met words often used
Understood but still confused
I felt what was often taken
For superficial actions and
Sometimes mistaken
Meanwhile I can't replace the love
I have for you
And feeling just ok
Everything remaining the same way
See, the learning
That's what gets me through my days
Sometimes soul searching
And taking time for oneself
Is the best thing
Realizing that both positive and negative experiences
Are Blessings

Now knowing, if nothing else
This one thing to be true
SOULMATE, I can see our ribbon in the sky
Even without seeing me and you

Open Book

Release me from pages
Of anticipation
Change the weight of my fears
With grips of hair
Finger licked pages
Turn me over
Size me up
Open this literary masterpiece
Stop skipping pages
Ignoring my text
I need you to cherish
What comes next
Send chills down my spine
Leather, untwined
Kiss me
Intoxicate my mind
And my body will follow
Beyond my cover is divine value
As detailed as my words
When you translate completely
Don't copy me

Learn what I'm about
Pursue an ending that never
Runs out
I'm your favorite
Open me and turn freely
These pages
Never let me forget

Time

Sweet time, give me more
Of what seems so divine
I stood in line
To feel more aligned
With you
Words spill rapidly and in sync with
Thoughts of what was meant to be
But what were we
Your love was questionable

The best things in life are without purpose
Or explanation
Then time cuts them short
Leave me to question the life
I grabbed by the experiences
Living vicariously through
All the breathtaking moments
To survive
My serenity came with time
And love came as a bonus

I hope to go back there some day
Not in time but in love
And see you smiling there
Until then, thank you for stopping for me
Time, thank you for stopping for us

Exclusive

I found myself encased
In such an intergalactic feeling
My milky way was in orbit
I was hot but had chills all over
Immediately drowning in
Never-ending amounts of beautiful black water
Water so dark
That even the latest of nighttime
Couldn't compare
I was paralyzed, tight
All invitations to arouse my eyes
With a glimpse of this ecstasy in human form
I declined
Eyes closed tight
Completely immobile
An hour and twelve minutes
And counting
And counting
And counting
Everything that was liquid was rushing
Everything that was imaginary
Soon became so real
As real as fingertips on new skin
As lovely as the sound of peace and serenity

As deep as poetry is for me
For experiences
Yet an act as temporary as time
Temporarily divine
An act exclusively mine
I STILL FEEL HIM

Tru Story

I care for
You
Maybe
Our love can
In utopia, be real
Only one
May have my Love
Solely
Real in composition
Never taken lightly
For you, time
May never fade
For us
A dream obtained
Are we sure
Have we come
Close to new
Are me and you defining true
Because if
It is to be
It is
Meant for we
Soulmate is in you, love
For life, sun, moon and stars

Combine your being

A tune for you

For I...

Poetic

Is this romantic's heart, soul and mind

I care for you

Maybe

My love can

In utopia be real

For us

Four Nineteen

An open heart is most vulnerable
When left open for you
To pour your salt
On complacent wounds
Like a closed door, not locked
But you won't go through
That four letter word so often used
Understood
But still confused
What do we have to lose
Pride perhaps, that's all I see
When can we be
We get closer to falling
Then further from us
Intertwined in lust and mistrust
We are stuck in
Organ's orbit

Someone Missed

At the peak of despair
Your soul listened
What I'd been missing
Was you
I find it hard to say
Us together is wrong
But I love our
Love song
Why can't we fly away
I can't share your wings anymore
Rose petals and diamonds
Our anniversary reborn
Your reciprocity excites my heart
Call it infatuation
Procrastination and encapsulated pride
Long distance love
Ignites me
Innocent eyes
Excite me
Hypnotize my reality in your absence
You plant seeds
That capture the trust in me
Lust for me intentionally
And make me long for
Our imminence

I Dedicate

Years pass
Time slows
Now a chance to relapse
And he says
WELCOME TO THE LAW SHOW
You're probably thinking
What once was love extinction
Is now a yellow light
But it's blinking
Slow down, but keep proceeding
While hate turns green with envy
They knew it
A love so strong it makes POWERFUL MUSIK
Breaking the endless cycle down
GET UP and go get love
As his glove fills with seven long years of tears
And pain
Whispers of "you can be my wife"
Swell his veins
Go deeper
While his HUSH GIRL fades
Back and forth
So, how are you
Why'd you leave

I love you
Who was he
Did you think of me after all this time
When I get what's mine
DON'T CROSS THE LINE
Blurred lines of love never drawn
Spent four years in agony
While he and I, not we, moved on
And a few times it was pure lust
But THERE YOU GO creating trust
Without us
Use our map, no LEGEND
And find where the journey ends
You are free to be you
Cocky, Intelligent, Sexy
And I AM ME
Funny, sweet and confident without conceit
We are the AMERICAN DREAM
So don't KEEP RUNNIN'
I know you are scared
But my actions carry the weight of my words
And if this love thing is for the birds
Well which one are you
Committed to show

I AM TRUTH

But if you choose to GO ON, when our time is NOW

Just promise to be back by sundown

Even if it's DRIVIN' ME INSANE

I'll be here until our love runs out

And then run out and refill it

Let it spill out on the pages of our story

Into the cracks beneath your feet

So you always walk with this love beat

CLOSE UR EYEZ and dream of your helpmate

As I proudly sing MY GOODBYE SONG

And celebrate fate

This man to this woman

This love to this hate

This lost to this found

This time to recreate

This old but so new

This chance to take

This pen to this paper

These words...

I DEDICATE

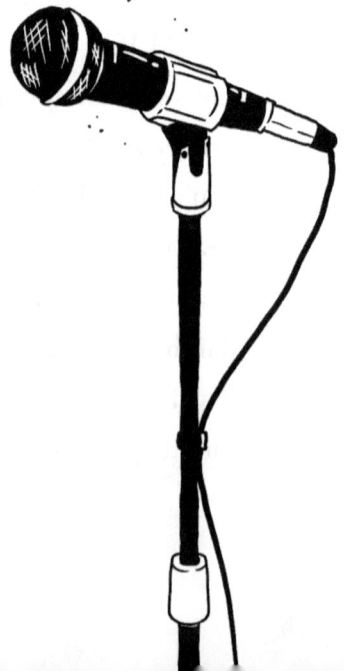

Love Birds

Fly with me
In order to see
What we can be
We have to
Leave this tree
Let God be
I believe
In the intentional
You and me
Omnipotently
We soar

Missed Moments

You are the best
Moment in my mind
A moment in time
Engulfed in divine destiny
I got so lost in love
Yearning for us
Lost in touch
From words on pages
And distance rushed
We lost so much
I regret that I couldn't reach you
I regret the moment I missed
To see you
Again

Penmanship

Why does ink run out
But the mind keeps writing
The story
I can't let him go
I said
I'll be sure
To let him know
I wrote
I love you
Unspoke
Just written in odes
In stanzas
In metaphors
In...

What Color Are We

Yellow
That comes to mind
When I think of
Us
It looks like
Bold energy
Exploding with radiant purpose
Different hues though
Bright or dim at times
Maybe we are
Blue
Like clarity
When you see through me
And I see you
But that changes sometimes too
Green
Seems more accurate
When we get mixed up in
What perfect looks like
But when guards are let down it's
White
Open, honest, trustworthy
It feels right
It's light and free

Changing the saturation

Giving us a tint of

What

Will

Always

Be

What color are we

God's Gift
Author's Ode

An angel of Grace
With pure innocence encased
Inside her, a beauty so deep
Unworthy of reach
She makes it hard to speak
Even when sentiment escapes
If she were to ever leave
Souls would stop searching
Longing to fulfill an overbearing need
For her
She's the type of woman
You want alongside you
Her grace brightens even the darkest
Of days
Without a word, just a look
Disarray
Her touch is soft, always
Appealing to your deepest thoughts and desires
She sets the bar high
And all minds inquire
Never compared, she is aware
Of her potential
Only one reason though

For why she exists
Simply explained in
A meaning of a name
She is truly
God's Gift

- CHAPTER II -

Fire

Suffocate

Stop walking around holding your breath

Shoulders high

Suffering

Teeth clinched

Settling

For death

Is looming

From suffocated words

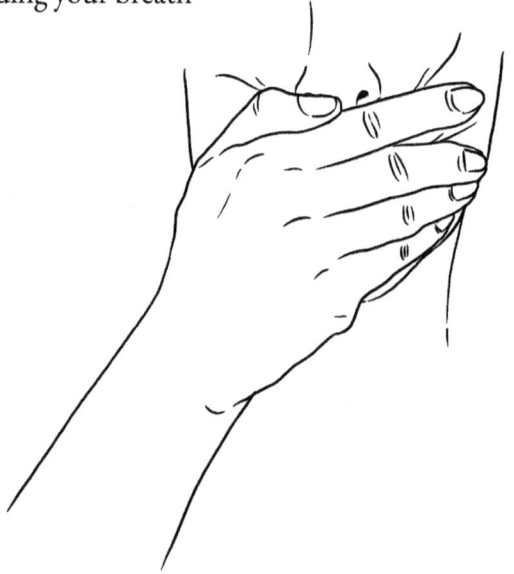

Restored

I am immune
To your distress
But have no regrets
You left me
New

Rising

I don't want nothing
Contingent
Nothing that's mediocre
Or in competition with
I don't want wasted time spent
I don't want what's not
Mine
According to divine
And I don't want the idea of
Time
To be your only association
With
My
Worth
I don't want fragmented
I don't want partial pieces
Where my entire soul
Is dissected to fill up your
Inequities
And
Discrepancies
And
Inconsistencies
Still remain

For reasons I don't even care
To entertain
I don't want undeserved
I don't want unpreserved
I don't want lack of awareness
Or spatial convolution
When I spelled out GENTLE
With
Good
Examples
Necessary
To
Learn
Each other
Where did you get less than
From anything that
Has to do with
Me
I don't want pity
Or projection
I don't want deflection
Or dissected non-negotiables
I don't want what most
Are willing to settle for

If it doesn't bring me peace
And disrupts my nervous system
Lastly
I don't want apologies
That start off with far-fetched feelings and
Lack of accountability
I hope gravity helps you
Rise to the purpose

Good Grief

I grieved selflessly
Making exchanges
For what valuable materials are
I grieved our misunderstandings
I was too responsible for
Demanding my worth
From you
The gift was
Life that controls the curse
Of losing my womb
I grieved your insecurities
The ones that abused
The fertility of my mind
Planting seeds of degradation
Watered with your legacy
I prayed for you and me
But unconditional expectations
Were too untimely and
Honesty was too high up
For you
We both paid a price
But I had more to lose
And you could never choose
Me

Self-careful

I need a manicure
But what time
Is there for relaxation
When I can't even
Think without interruption
My thoughts don't
Have the liberty to
Sprint through my mind
Without waiting
For the right time
To be heard
Don't use your voice though
It's not humble enough
To free words
It's not ok
To stumble through
What comes first
You cannot say
What you mean
You make it worse
Don't talk
Don't breathe
Stay inside yourself
Or you will scream

Keep it together
Why can't you just
Keep it together
Why can't you just
Think better
Why can't you just
Pick a color
Less
Outspoken

First

If love is patient
Why do you rush me
To change
If love is kind
Why do you lose your softest words
When I need them most
If love does not envy
Why are you so critical of me
Do not boast your shame
I am proud of the arrival
But regret the distance we came
If love is not rude
Why is it so hard to recover
From the truth
There is no M in We
Until we are upside down
In emotional greed
And I pity the outcome
Every time
We don't belong angry
Yet we flee from
Our most fulfilling memories
To prove that sorrow is the
Sugar coated wrapper

Love is not resentful
But I can't recover from
Falling asleep to
Calculations of what you meant
To say
If love never fails
Why do I often wonder
Where it went

All This Time

A cold space
Scolded with constant
Disappointment
From never meeting
The expectations of your
Idea of us
The conceptual unity
Moving through
Love
And
Lust
Contentment is the instigator
Of what we must
Do
We are confined to
Speak our truth
Appropriately
Burned authenticity and
Unavoidable silence
Navigating
The beginning and the end
All this time

Trap-estry

This is my confession
A masterpiece of
Hard lessons learned
I cross-stitched
The best parts of my existence
For you
And you dishonored me ·
You created an intricate
Tapestry of my frailty
Trust and honesty
Were neutral colors
Completely optional
The physical characteristics of your aura
Disguised your noxious being
Like a piece of art
Our meaning bounced back and forth
Depending on the angle
I lost each pattern you were
You are woven
Of fabricated textures
Insulated by guilt
Embellished with deceptive details
Patterned with narcissism
You are a futile concept
A calico of lies

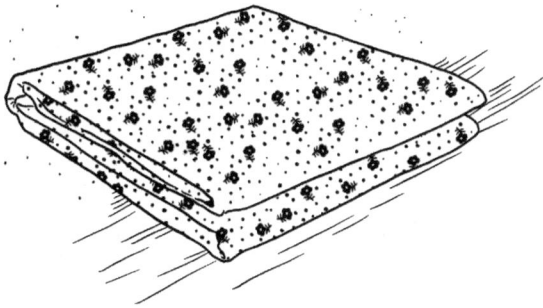

One on One

The prototype from afar
A distant
Superstar
A love game
We played
And you leveled up hard
And I lost track of
How much of
My time you wasted
You grew so complacent
Adjacent to our seasons
End

Lost Coordinates

There is nothing to celebrate with you

I am convenient

And your idea of us

Is obsolete

I get it now

Why we should have never been

To be grateful

Is to be shamed and humiliated

It is to be

A great fool

We are coasting

Great

Fool

Ungrateful you are

Where we are heading

Is nowhere together

Look how far we have

Gone

Until Dawn

Dawn came
And I realized
I stayed up all night
Confirming my grief
Entangled in your web of misconception
Longing for the truth
At the tip of your tongue
That you let slip
So easily through your fingertips
For others
I stayed up despite
Your public condemnation of my character
I stayed up
Bleaching away your illusion
Of me
I stayed up
Ridding myself
Of every
Single
Part
Of
You
I stayed up to say goodbye

Plans

I used to think I could fly
Passed the stars
To reach you
I dreamed you
Would come back
To me
I missed you on Mars
Where the air is heavy
And mountains are
Covered in laurels
I forgot what
The ground felt like
I traveled too far
Beyond stars
It was hard
When you left me
And death meant
You'd forget me
I regret you kept me
Away

Everywhere and KNOWwhere

I couldn't wait to tell you
That you don't deserve me
But instead
I said that
I don't deserve peace
I said that
I don't deserve me
Every time I called out for you
With dependency
See
With you
I have this tendency to forget
What makes sense to me
Like what time of day
Or season
Or reason
I find your toxicity
Most palatable
Chasing the why made me
Lose pieces of my sanity
I searched for them all
Over and under
And everywhere
And they wouldn't fit

Together
So, I gave you a call
To help me make sense
Of why
To trim down painful edges
And force odd feelings
Shaped like honeycombs
Into tiny, sticky little voids
But you didn't answer
And I didn't
Know where to go
To recover

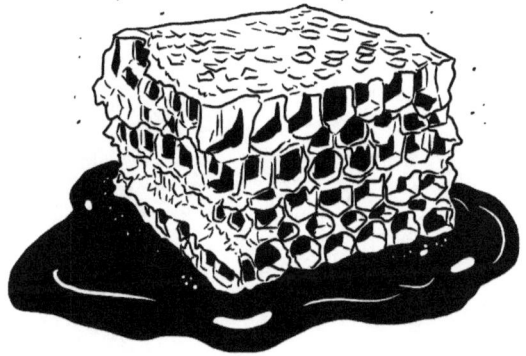

Goodbye

You look happy now
I'm glad we found a route
In opposite directions

Discernment

Discernment is
Nothing short of a Blessing
It saved me from
Embarrassment
It reminded me
What your words lacked
Syllables without act
Empty promises without
The longevity to sustain
What brought us back
Off and on
And off
Track
Discernment is
The lasting impression
Of a disappointing memory
And your attempts to engrain me
With
Resentment

Hush

Stop speaking to me as if
I don't exist
As if to say my being
Lacks common sense
And consciousness
Is a puddle of
Muddled words
And dissonance
Where I struggle to be
Heard
And you're not interested
Stop seeing me
Without being me
Without needing and feeding
Me
That's not to say
I pray for the day you
Believe in me
But you can't even see
Where I keep transparency
Tucked away like a
Gradual transition from
Monday to Sunday
And mundane
Becomes my way of life

Stop speaking to me
Unless you are prepared
For accountability
I don't keep account of
Transgressions
But my ability to decipher your
Intentions
Is like measuring assets against liabilities
And I'm not discounting
Your hypocrisy
Stop speaking to me without
Certainty
Without being convinced that
Every syllable has to convey
Only what is most important
And impactful for me to stay
Invested
Like this exchanging of words
Is more than filling in the emotional blanks
Of scantrons
Until tested
Stop speaking to me
Stop speaking to me
Stop speaking to me
And listen

Daydreams

Sometimes I feel like
We're only better
When we run from each another
It's like
At least we are willing to go the
Distance
For instance, there's always a past crease
In your back pocket
That disrupts my peace
And your piece of mind isn't
For keeps
But I still like the way you look
When you sleep
It's never that deep
And that bothers me
Sometimes we don't try
We just pick up where we left off
And then wonder why we
Cry about it later
Sometimes I can't stand going
From great to greater
Because I know it'll be short lived
And you'll hate that you
Stayed to see what happens

After the credits
I wish I could say most often
Sometimes sounds so half filled
Like taking a few sips of bliss
And a few bites of anguish
Is filling enough
Is balanced enough
To stay for a little while longer
And eat the regret
You can only swallow
If you cut it smaller
Sometimes I can't go anywhere
But without you feels better too
And that's hard to wake up from

Edge

I write
To be set
Free
Everything I scribe
I see around me

Tough Times

I miss you because
I love you
And I'm not quite sure
Which one
I regret more

Shame On You

Shame on you
For being everything
You said you wouldn't
And would
As a mother
Shame on you
For withstanding
The very existence of
Societies disapproval
Shame on you
For standing up
And down
And within
And sound
To make sure you
Stay the course
Intended
Shame on you
For not detouring
From your divine path
Shame on you
For making something
Impossible happen
Shame on you

For fitting a square
Into a circle
Day in
And
Day out
Shame on you
For being
Remarkable

Lost Sight

I didn't see it coming
I counted on you
But you have still let me down
And maybe
In some ways
We have
Each other
In the moments where we let
Resentment and past experiences
Be a restriction on our potential
Or
Maybe we made all of this up
And in the next lifetime
You won't have my eyes to look into

Ruined

I was ruined
One day I was
Fooled into believing
A nice gesture
Was
A safe space
Because
God made me
Unconditional
God gave me
Light and compassion
And love
And God knew I would share
In his likeness

One day I was ruined

But not like
Broken edges
Of rocks and artifacts
But ruined like
Tarnished molecules

Of a soul's sediment
That drifted somewhere
It didn't belong
Like rare stones
Ground and garnished
Into dust
Then into nothing
Then swept away
By time moving forward

One day I was ruined

Into the distance
I went searching for
Disappearance
I longed for
And found after
Searching under my small frame
For statistics
That say
I could be validated
For probable causes

That say
I would be less ashamed
And more likely to be
Rebuilt and replanted
And revised
And relieved
And recreated
And reciprocated
And watered
Eventually

One day I was abandoned

And the choice between
Two evils
Making it home safe
Or becoming another
Silenced, shamed, humiliated
Woman
Seemed to be the lesser of the two
And a lesson
In who

Predators are
Or maybe
Shiny primates
That prey on light
And yet somehow
Making it home
Just ruined me more
And that hurts me to my
Core

One day I was ruined

Somehow
If I had just
Kept walking
Oblivious to an open window
And the smell of cheap cologne
The fragment of the moon
Warning me of the darkness to come
I could have
Reached out

And asked for help
Or sent a distress signal
For someone to question
Which direction I withered

One day I was ruined

And I will never recover

- CHAPTER III -

Melanin

The Greatest
Goat Talk

What's a GOAT
The greatest
You can't dispute that
I'm the most hated
Never underrated
And don't debate it
I'm like Ali
When I see Red
I turn your blue black
In the kitchen I'm bakin' and shakin'
I'm Tom Brady
When the skin snap
Plus, I been THAT
These words are anointed
Each syllable is God's Gift
Like HOV is
When they ask
I tell them
God did
Verbal racket
Like Serena
I'm your favorite
I cut though barriers

And records

I'm serrated

Top of the leader board

I'm SURE rated

You don't even want the score

Like Jordan when he said I'm finished

Then he gave us

Six more

And my time ain't near

It's right HERE

Like Babe

The ceiling is glass

The "roof" (RUTH) always been clear

Like Ye

You're in my class

Ain't no dropout near

I'm a Monster

I'm a poet

I'm a walking entendre

We Are

We are monolithically regal
Rarely given due credit in the
Big picture
Indebted to a society
That deems us inferior
In the grand scheme of things
Living while Black
Is being content with
What good luck brings
To love hate back
Concedes our dignity
We are excused from equality
Resiliency is our childhood
We are not our oppressors
Because we are shackled by our regression
Disproportionately and systemically
Contested, arrested
And undervalued
On the cusp of peace
Is an uprising
Uniting and still disguising
Our protest of injustices
In a manner that is favorable for you
We are confined to accepting

That even our hurt

Is not good enough

We cannot clean up your chaos

Because we always

Miss a spot

Racism is taught

But our ancestors fought

Tirelessly

Inspired by free

The recoil

Is no longer in our DNA

GLORY

The Mask Wears Us

The mask inhabits our face
Like air molecules into our melanin
It's existence is definite, yet disguised
By family values and carpe diem cries
Truth is the sigh
Of living
Continued through the grief of existence
After Blessings are exhausted from not being exalted
Comfortable with the mask, all experiences become un-new
This mask we wear takes all forms of face
And those who preach through judgement
Have lost their protected space
Truth grins bear all under it's skin
And make room for freedom
We are used by our mask to save
Being who we are
What's under the mask we wear
What has gotten us this far
Why hide behind hardships
With righteousness inside
Why cover our truths
And let others read lies
From our faces of shame
Pour tears of pride

With lack of faith in our hearts
Close behind
We are running out of time
Disguised by a mask
We wear fear
Transparency, bring us home
Set us free

The Bare Sole

They'll say it was a
Coup
The resistance
There is power in
Injustice
And in
Justice
We soothe our
Bare feet
With
Aloe
Our path remains
Rubbled yet steady
We are
Bruised yet Blessed
Unbroken
We are upright
We are aflame
On purpose

Reborn

This is the application of
My insecurities
Manifested into my wildest dreams
My destiny
Has been reborn
Nothing is or was – what it seemed
I am a new creation
Redeeming my faults
Intentionally grasping my potential
With two hands

Too Political

My eyes have seen the glory
Of the coming of a liar
Stuffy, golf resort, country club, overnight-stay buyer
Doesn't relate to mothers and fathers
Brothers and sisters
American troops dying
Their generations crying
A winner in his own sins
A sinner in his own grins
Using generations as puppets of dirt
Their sacrifice worthwhile
Addressing the nation with
Vindictive trials
Minorities exiled
Battles for restoration
Un-won
Losses suffered,
Murders and oppression
Un-done

Melanin Girl

Beige

Black

Brown

Downtown vibes

Hazel

Toffee

Caramel

Around the way eyes

Doobie wrap

Kinky hair girl

Alphabet curls

We run this world

Girly

Masculine

With a feminine spin

Perfect smile

Worth ANY while

You are supreme

Soulful magic

You are vintage

Classic

A queen

Oppressed
The Glory

Beaten

Bruised bodies

That embody

Your appropriations

We are good enough

For lyrics and recreations

Yet we must

Create our own

Reparations

By breaking generational curses

From prisons

And hearses

To hands up don't shoot

And bible verses

Used against us

God is for all people

And he meant it

We are exalted

Yet still at oppressions disposal

We are exhausted

And supposed to be grateful

After all the light

It costs us

Gripped by racisms curse

But even in darkness

We are

The glory

Criminal

We are

Ignited by unequal

On fire

From unspeakable

Crimes against us

Dehumanized by

Attempts to eliminate

Our DNA

You control us

With a system designed

To ghost us

We must

Rise

Just Us

By any means
We must fight
Righteousness
Is
Light

Black

I'm a Black woman
And a Black mom
And a Black poet
On my Black grind
I got Black time
To talk Black crime
You hear Black cries
That's a Black sign
Let's talk Black lives
You sell Black lies
When my Black size
Equals Black demise
And your colorless views
That makes Blacks sigh
But our regal skin
Now that's Black prime
That's no Black surprise
You hate Black pride
You hate Black minds
You hate Black shine
I have Black kids
I'm a Black wife
I have Black friends
We talk Black strife

We speak Black wealth
We ARE Black wealth
We need Black resources
For our Black health
We need Black history
On our Black shelves
So, we can never forget
How Black is spelled
We say Blacks unite
You see Blacks rebel
Our only ally, is our stories
That are Black as well
This is a Black fight
Protest
Black rights
And when we make it to the top
We scream BLACK LIVES

Victory

Victory is in the
Recoding of
Generational molding
Used to sustain the
Shame of being
It is the control of circumstance
Victory is upbringing
Washed away
To birth a new mindset
It is time spent
Recovering from
Silence
Victory is freedom

Victory is in your DNA
How you speak and think
Lay foundation for
Triumph
Victory is David
no Goliath
Victory is faith

Victory is the will
To transcend darkness
From beginning to end
And rise above
Assigned affinity of circumstances
Victory is defiance
Of worthlessness and defeat
Victory is as we speak

The Victor slays the tyrant
Of their destiny
They behead their
Oppressive paralysis
The Victor is the challenger
Relentless
Resilient
It is the peace of perspective
The Victor is the message

Normality

Let's normalize
Not telling me my distress
Is normal
That as long as I'm in
Fight or flight
I'm alive despite
My body surviving
Quarrel
Let's normalize
Seeing me
Not just grazing over
My features
And tone of voice
To be categorized
As a conflict
To your expertise
Where you forget
To acknowledge why I'm even here
And I won't dare
Speak up
Because you know better than me
Let's normalize
My heartbeat
My lungs

My sanity
My tongue
The real chief complaint
Is how many times I've bit it
From restraint
Quietly suffering in silence
While I wait my turn
To debate
That I object your dissonance
But I'm never called upon

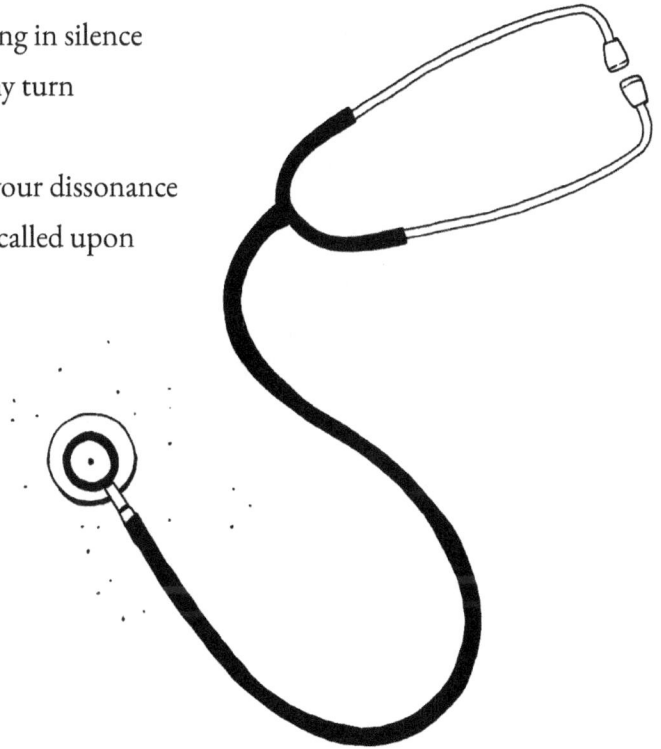

Black Anxiety

The hypocrisy of healing
Is that
It is for everyone
Except us
That somehow
We should have
Done better
Sought better
Chose better
Thought better
We should have
Fought better
We would have
Gotten better
Quicker
We could have
Saw you coming
But instead
We are depressed
Unpacking our post traumatic stresses
Over Airbnb rejections
For skin complexion
We have moved beyond
Regression

Our names aren't even

Enough for LinkedIn dreams

And it seems

We are better off doing things

By any means

Like Streams

Like Teams

Daydreams of light beams

And mainstream equality

Black is the snapped rope

Of hope

We are the anomaly

Beyond woke

Protesting injustice and

Looting to end justice

That kills us

Anxiously dodging

Skin folk

We are soul broke

To cope

Is to be rejected

To be redeemed

To be aggressive

To seek suppression

As a means to
Be respected
Anxiously objective
Retrospect besets us
This is
Black Anxiety

Rise Up

We pray
Yet still remain stagnant
Engulfed in malignant thoughts
Of reformation
Of transformality
How do we
Exchange our fear for legacy
And build the blueprint
of our dreams
How do we
Make sense of
Drive plus divine ratios
That equate to our
Most majestic outcomes
How do we
Rise up

HUEman

Brown is the color of unheard

And unseen

Unequivocal

Unrelenting

Undone

Unsurpassed

Brown is the color of

We

He

She

I

Them

They

And

Free

Brown is rest assured

And rested upon

Brown is reliable

Resilient

Resurrected and responsible

Brilliant

Brown is the color of

Collaboration

Creativity

And

Continuity

Brown is

You

Iridescent excellence

In true form

Brown is HUEman

Peculiar Fruits Of Our Labor

Like a bruised apple
Longing to be remembered
We wait for our time
Bittersweet-like lemon drops
The honey
Is between what was
And is to be
The roots of a tree unwatered
Is it not organic
To fall freely
Like oranges on
Their way to be
Commodity
Somehow disposed of
Instead
For natural selection
Is a sad dream
What a laborious thing
Peculiar fruits

A Lantern

What happens when
You light a match
And fire spreads
Much like when
You read a book
And knowledge heads
Into the minds
Of young and old
Alike
And like lightening
Ideas strike
Within a community
But which is faster
Does it matter
If you protest
Peacefully
Before or after
They take your rights
Away
Under or over
A broken bridge
Of truth
And dissonance
Tangled in warped

Misunderstandings
And political
Righteousness
And right when
You think there's a break
In convoluted clouds
Of perceived injustices
You, I or perhaps
We
Are subject to a
Massacre of historical
Reckoning
Much like pages
Being torn out and beheaded
Like books without spines
Words scrambled in piles
Of positional persecution
Alphabet ashes
Where are the safes
Full of chapters
Instead of currency
Locked up for safe keeping
Like a lantern
That never burns out

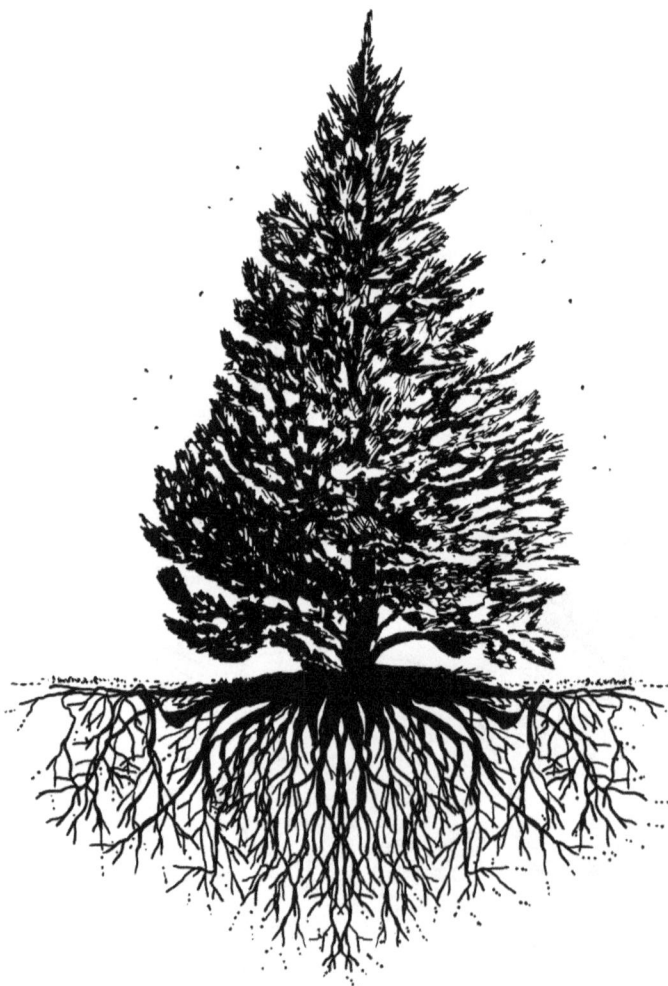

- CHAPTER IV -

Soul

Oh To Be a Mother

Oh to be a Mother
To discover
That each time you give life
It is a new opportunity to
Uncover your strength
Who are you child
Who will you be
Are you a reflection of
Me
Don't seek my approval
Be proud of yourself
First
Apply your gifts for greater works
This once tiny seed
That grows
That changes
That strives
That survives
The confines of
A society that determines
When you should be heard, seen and acknowledged
Oh to be a Mother
Unplugging the cords
Of generational expectations

Ripping up the weeds of excuses
For your examples of turning out just fine
I hear you calling my name
The subtle corrections
From a tiny yet powerful
Voice
Tell me when I'm wrong
Speak your truth
Oh to be a mother

Pride

I wear this cape
Proudly
Although sometimes it
Drowns me
With
Regret
Anticipation of what's yet to come
There are a million and one things to do
But I get them done
I sometimes shun
Offers for help
Because I have checked my entire
Tank
And have fumes left to offer
Thanks
For all you have helped me through

INNERState

Let's go
Somewhere
We can plan
As we go
And grow
Up there
Take pictures
Of the landscape
Who we know
Up there
I'm hungry
But I can't
Feed my soul
Until
We share
Growing old
A single pair
On
What's this road
Where to
I know
Where

Poet

A poet is a friend of words
A dream of verbal constellations
A light of instance
A poet is epiphany

Be Well

Barefoot feet on grass
My toes
Compose the symphony
Of mindfulness
Sensations of what is
Beneath me
Graciously release me
Ground my spirit
In healing
And catapult me
Into wellness

HeartFULL

I need you to protect me
Even when you
Regret me
I need you to forget me
Don't let me mislead you
Anymore
Why are you always complacent
When I ignore you
But you thrive
If I adore you
I can't restore you
To full capacity
I can't respond
When you ask for me
Anymore

Being

We sway back and forth
Exuding the freedom to
Exist
Both present and projecting
We search for a means to
Be still
To experience our truths
Uninterrupted by expectation
While love for all things
Persists

The Fog

I walked around in a fog
No one could see me or hear my pain
I walked around in a fog
Waiting for it to rain
Such a sad, lonely
Dense aura
Sweeping around my mind
Loudness of my sorrows because
I'm running out of time
I walked around in this fog
Over and over again
Still, I couldn't figure out
Where does it begin and end
I thought I saw someone who knew
And as I started to ask
You ran right by me without a word
Reminding me why we live but never last
This fog it gives me something
I never knew I had
The wetness of my tongue from words
I wish I hadn't said
I walked around in a fog today
I even sometimes ran
But there was not a single one

To take my weary hand
Not even you were in the mist
Waiting on the other end
I walked around in a fog a while
Until tomorrow's end

Reflection

"I see you"
She said to herself
And only time, which is of the essence
Will determine why the cards
Dealt to her
Are played as such
You see, she can't quite understand why she cries so much
Or why she hides behind the lies seen right though her eyes
When the times get tough
But whatever it is, is enough
To break her down
You see she's given and taken evenly
Hurt and been hurt unspeakably
Yet loved hard and been loved unconditionally
Cringing at giving herself often so freely
Coming from the only place she feels safe
A place outside of herself
Encouraged to let people know that
Each day passing
Is a day never re-lived
Nothing lasts forever
Her transparency is fearless
"I see you"
She said to herself

And only time, which is of the essence
Will determine why the cards
Dealt to her
Are played as such
"I see you"
I said to myself
As I stepped back from the mirror
Quickly realizing
I don't recognize her anymore

Anxiety

Thank you
For coming and going
As you please
You give me permission
To sit in grief
You are turmoil and peace
I need you to succeed
I feel you
Beneath my feet
Right before my next step
Into reality

IntentionALL

Bright beams
Of light
Take flight
Dreams in site
Despite fright
Night seems
Polite
Frees my soul
Can't close my eyes
On goals
On life
Through strife
With all my might
Damn right
I fight

Author

An author
Is many things
Both child and adult
Both complex and
Still void of intricacy
An author sees words
As the bridge between
Here and there
On surface and
All around
Authors hear sound as
Alphabets in symphony
In C, G or E
What instrument most
Breathes my thoughts
Captivating their audience with
Elusive tension
And exclusive conception of idea
Authors make us wonder
Where we are going and
How will we get there
An author is many things
All but
Silent

Yield

I'm full of words
But nothing to say
I can write you a map
But can't tell you the way
Please
Don't
Stay

At Ease

Solitude
Is my peace
I am at ease
When I am
With me
I can't see
What is missing
Or what is empty
I don't think
Of how much
Heartache has
Sent me
Or that
Loneliness has
Befriended me
Or that my mind
Can't complete a
Thought
All that I am
I can't be
I escape
Reality
My disdain
For

Time heals all things

Does not distract me

My intentions

Don't battle me

When

Solitude is

In me

I am at ease

Empty

Passer By

I crossed paths
With a lady at the store
And she said,
You look like you're going places
And I had to reflect back
Because as a matter of fact
I am
Perplexed
You see
I just got my life
Together
In fact
If better was a season
It took me decades to
Weather the storm
I'm talking submerged
For no reason
Like never wanted to
Lose myself
But amber alerted
My entire being
And for
No good reason

You see
In that tiny micro-moment
She just knew
That I had reached my peak
But what she didn't see
Is how decades prior
I used to fight
For syllables
But wouldn't dare speak
My truth
I used to feel like
If I keep settling for less
Then eventually life's complexities
Will start to add up
Like once I'm rich with regret
And wealthy with self-doubt
I'll be able to pay back
All the fulfillment I borrowed
From other people

I was off topic
So much so
That I had to write about it
And turn it into

Entertainment
So I didn't cry about it
Didn't die about it
I never lie about it though
Because it made me
Resilient
But in 2016 I almost
Lost my life
And from that came
Deep pain
And the last month of the year
Doesn't feel the same
Never has
Never will

I smiled though
When the lady asked me
If I'm always this happy
Because six years prior to that
I was walking on glass
And giving life was the only
Thing that just happened to be
Crystal clear
And just prior to that I left my soul

To chase my heart
To follow my mind
To miss divine
When he was mine
Because time made me feel better
The delays
Made it all
A little easier to weather

I was wondering if I had
Lost sight of my identity
Or if I could only see
What that did to me
And not him
More like if I keep
Stepping outside of myself
Out of body experiences
Won't feel like they are really
My possessions
And shame will be separate
And I won't seem so desperate
For understanding

And that lady didn't even know me
But I know she saw me
For who I am
Who I was
And who I will be
She told me she can't wait
To read my books
And that meant a lot
I'm glad I managed to stay on topic
And I'm glad she
Passed me by

Beware

Beware of people who say
That you "do too much" getting after anything
You pour too much
You excel too much
You shine too much
You propel too much
Each goal you accomplish will be of no use
To them

Pocketed Feelings

Pocketed feelings
Sometimes rise
Like buildings
With sky-scraped intentions
Made of rubble and loose particles
Admirable indeed
The way they fit
And intertwine
City streets
And winding pathways
Of suppression and silence
You can walk up to them
Standing tall
Or small
Or elongated with
What seems like decades of
Immeasurable timelines
Pocketed feelings
Extend the minds structure
They bend the hearts
Foundation
With all their new
Blueprints
And plans to reinvent themselves
To give us something new
Next go round

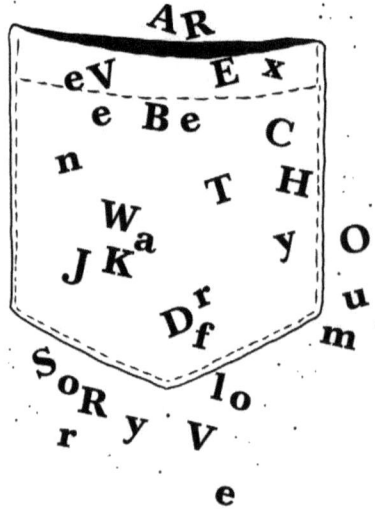

A Compass

Intention
Is the road to
Unanswered prayers
Conviction
Is how long
The journey

Ideas

Ideas are a comrade
Of time
A seeker of sixty seconds
To plan
An act of impact
Ideas are like circuits
That have charge
At both ends
When to start
And where to plug in
No beginning
And
No end
Just infinite

Loneliness

Loneliness is fickle
So much so
That even a trickle
Of turbulence
Can cause an avalanche
That even a riot
Can erupt
From protested positions
And picketed conjuring
Of doubt
Loneliness feels like
All five senses are
Void

Word To The Wise

When words come
Capture them
Write them down
Piece them together
Pulling from verbal
Curves and nuances
And innuendos
To find a subject that
Feels balanced
To find the right
Cadence
When words come
Savor the syndicated
Syllables
That don't yet
Have labels of logic
Until they find their
Conjunction
Until they become
Sisters in stanza
When words come
Cherish them
Understand that to share them
Is to command

The eyes and ears

Attention

When words come

Look and listen

For relationship

When words come

Sync the fragmented journey

Until sunrise

How Far To Home

I traveled far and long today
I landed in front of a coffee shop
Many people passed by
But none stopped
I thought
No one sees me, I know
How far to home

At times I lost my way
In and out of travelers' paths
Some were kind
Some were cruel
To most I was invisible
No one needs me, I know
How far to home

As weather turned from bright to gray
I nestled in a corner
Disheveled from the journey
Exhausted from destiny sowed
I am alone
No one reads me, I woe
How far to home

If I met a friend, what would I say
I've lost my words
Will you lift me up
We can go on a never-ending journey
This way
When someone shows me, I grow
How far to home

A gust of hope then carries me away
Into the path of a passerby's reach
Kept neatly by one's kindness
My story starts the journey
My purpose is restored
Someone freed me, finally
Not far to
Home

About The Author

Mashao has long dreamed of becoming a published author, a journey that began when she started writing poetry and short stories at just eight years old. What once was a quiet refuge became a lifelong calling. Several decades later, *Pages of Plenty* was born—a heartfelt collection meant to inspire readers who find meaning in both life's optimism and the power of shared experience and community. *Pages of Plenty* is the blossoming of a journey: a tapestry of reflection, hope, and shared humanity. Her poetry is a balm, a mirror, a melody—and above all, a gift. For Mashao, poetry has always been both an emotional outlet and a source of healing. There is no greater reward than sharing her words with others. *Pages of Plenty* is more than a book—but a path walked together. And as always, it is all for you.

○ @pagesofplenty

www.ingramcontent.com/pod-product-compliance
Lightning Source LLC
Chambersburg PA
CBHW072350090426
42741CB00012B/2997

The authors of *Mount and Mountain* invite the reader to learn from and reflect on essential issues that come from the well-spring of the Ten Commandments. Their discussions are filled with passion and insight as they both challenge and learn from their own Jewish and Christian traditions as well as from each other. They grapple with Scripture, spirituality, history, and philosophy as they consider how ancient words and tradition continue to move and to confront us today.

—*Sharon Pace*
Associate Professor of Hebrew Bible/Judaica
Marquette University
Author of *Daniel* (Smyth & Helwys Bible Commentary)

In a Southern Christian culture that tends to prefer public idolizations of the Ten Commandments over actually listening to and heeding them, a Baptist minister sits down with a rabbi—in the heart of Tennessee—to help each other better hear and understand. While remaining true to their respective (and in this case overlapping) traditions, Rev. Michael Smith and Rabbi Rami Shapiro demonstrate humility, honesty, and respect as they plow together the always fertile soil of this most sacred ground. Come. Sit. Listen in. And learn to trust the Divine Author, as do the minister and the rabbi, to water and nurture in you a deeper understanding and appreciation of these ten words to His children.

—*Bert Montgomery*
Author of *Psychic Pancakes & Communion Pizza* and
Elvis, Willie, Jesus & Me